Dedication

To Mary Beth—
Whose faithful love has reflected God's grace in every season, and to the Lord, whose mercy continues to shape our story beyond what we could have imagined.

Living Out
the Lord's Supper

Why Being at the Table Is Just the Beginning

J. Brian Pusateri

Acknowledgments

This book is the fruit of many quiet conversations, prayers, and faithful friendships over the years.

I am deeply grateful to my wife, Mary Beth, whose steady faith and honest love have strengthened every chapter of our shared life. Our children and grandchildren remain among God's greatest gifts to me, and their grace and encouragement have shaped this journey more than they know.

I am thankful for the many individuals who read early drafts of this manuscript and offered thoughtful insight, careful critique, and generous encouragement. Their willingness to engage the message helped refine both the clarity and the heart of these pages.

I am also grateful for the countless people across the country and around the world who have shared their stories with me through Broken Door Ministries. Their courage, humility, and desire to grow have continually reminded me that what God does in us is always meant to flow through us.

Above all, I give thanks to the Lord, whose mercy has sustained this work and whose grace continues to shape every unfinished part of my life.

Contents

Preface

Christians around the world approach the Lord's Supper in different ways. We use different words, follow different traditions, and practice it within different rhythms of worship. Yet across those differences, something unites us. We gather at the table because we believe it matters. We come because Jesus invited His disciples to remember Him, to receive what He offered, and to carry that gift forward into their lives.

But many believers quietly wrestle with a question that lingers beneath the surface:

What is meant to happen after we receive?

Christians view and practice the Lord's Supper differently. Despite these differences, faith is present, and belief is sincere. What unites believers across these traditions is a shared question: how does the table shape the life that follows? For many, that connection can feel unclear.

This book begins with a simple conviction: the Lord's Supper was never meant to be an ending. It was meant to be a beginning.

On the night He gathered with His disciples, Jesus did

something strikingly simple. He took bread, blessed it, broke it, and shared it. Those movements reveal more than a moment in Scripture. They reveal a pattern — a rhythm meant to shape how believers understand their identity, their healing, and their calling in the world

We are taken — chosen by God and held in His hands.

We are blessed — met with mercy we did not earn.

We are broken and wounded — by our own failures and by life in a fallen world.

And we are shared — sent outward so that what God has done in us might bring hope to others.

This pattern does not belong to one denomination or tradition. It belongs to the Christian life itself. Wherever believers gather at the table, this rhythm quietly waits to be lived.

Many Christians sense this but struggle to put words to it. Faith can remain inward. Healing can feel incomplete. Growth can feel stalled. The table is honored, yet its deeper invitation remains unexplored. This book was written for those moments — for believers who long for a faith that moves beyond remembrance and becomes a way of life.

Rather than focusing on theological differences, this book focuses on a shared calling. It explores how the pattern revealed at the Lord's Supper speaks to everyday life — how it invites honesty rather than secrecy, community rather than isolation, and a life shared rather than a faith kept private.

This is not a book about striving harder or becoming someone else. It is about recognizing what God is already doing and allowing that work to move outward through us. It is an invitation to see the table not only as something we approach, but as something we carry.

The Lord's Supper reminds us of who we are.

It shows us how grace meets us.

And it sends us into the world changed.

Being at the table was never the end.

It was only the beginning.

CHAPTER ONE
When Everyone Else Looks Fine

Sunday mornings have a way of making us believe that everyone else has life figured out. We file into church dressed nicely and smiling, greeting one another in the hallway, settling into our favorite seats. From a distance, it looks like a community of confident, steady Christians who showed up ready to worship. If someone had taken a photograph of the congregation at that moment, most of us would look peaceful, composed, and put together. But photographs can be deceiving. They capture faces, not stories. They show expressions, not burdens.

If we could see beneath the surface of those Sunday morning smiles, we might discover something else entirely. We might find a young father silently worried about losing his job, a woman grieving a diagnosis she hasn't yet spoken aloud, a teenager carrying the weight of social pressure, or a couple barely holding their marriage together. We might see someone battling a temptation they've wrestled with for years, someone longing for forgiveness, or someone who feels invisible even while surrounded by people they love. We might encounter someone still carrying the scars of childhood trauma. We might even see a person who appears cheerful in every outward way but quietly feels spiritually numb, wondering why their faith seems to be moving in reverse.

The truth is, there is no person in any sanctuary who is completely untouched by brokenness or woundedness. Some of us recognize it readily. Others would never use those words to describe themselves. But whether we see it or not, every one of us carries something. Some carry the weight of choices they regret, choices that have left a mark on their lives. Others carry wounds they never asked for and never deserved, wounds inflicted by the loss of someone precious, by the betrayal of someone trusted, or by the harsh circumstances of living in a broken and unpredictable world.

Brokenness and woundedness are not the same thing, yet they live side by side in the human heart. Brokenness grows from the mistakes we make, the sins we commit, and the patterns we fall into again and again. It shows up in the ways we speak sharply when we meant to be gentle, the temptations we thought we had defeated only to find them returning, or the resolve that fades the moment we walk out of church. These are the places where we know we've contributed to our own struggles, where we wish we had acted differently, and where we quietly wonder if God is disappointed in us.

Woundedness, on the other hand, grows from the things that happen to us. These are the moments when life shifts in ways we never expected and never wanted. A child's accident. A spouse's illness. The slow ache of grief that lingers for years after a funeral. The sudden collapse of a friendship that once felt unshakeable. The loneliness that arrives without warning and stays longer than we hoped. The lingering ache of childhood traumas. These wounds are not our fault, yet they settle deep within us, shaping our fears, our hopes, and sometimes even our faith.

Some people readily acknowledge their brokenness. They know the struggles they face. They can describe the patterns that trip them up every time. But many people have difficulty recognizing or admitting the wounds they carry. Pain has a way of convincing us to stay silent. Grief teaches us to whisper. Trauma makes us bury the story so deeply that we sometimes forget it is still shaping our hearts. Even people whose lives appear calm and orderly on the surface may be carrying wounds that have never been spoken aloud.

This book is not written only for people who feel wounded, nor is it written just for those who recognize their brokenness. It is written for every believer who longs for a more authentic walk with Christ but sometimes finds themselves wondering why transformation seems slow or why certain struggles refuse to disappear. It is written for the person who has confessed the same sin a thousand times yet cannot seem to escape its shadow. It is written for the one who believes in God's love but has difficulty believing that His mercy could reach the hidden corners of their own heart. And it is written for those who feel strong and steady, who may not yet realize how the quiet places of their lives are shaping them in ways they have never examined.

Over the years, as I've interacted with countless people seeking to grow in their faith, I began noticing a consistent pattern. People often confessed their struggles to God but rarely spoke about them to anyone else. They prayed about their temptations. They felt guilty after failing. They asked God for forgiveness, sincerely and wholeheartedly. Yet they remained stuck. And the longer they stayed silent, the more their struggles tightened around them, as though secrecy itself gave their battles strength.

I began to understand that silence has a way of convincing us that we are alone, and loneliness has a way of convincing us that we cannot change. But something remarkable happens when a person begins to speak their truth out loud. When a man admits the pattern he has been hiding for years, something shifts inside him. When a woman finally names the grief she has carried since childhood, the heaviness in her chest begins to lift. When a teenager opens up about the fear they have been pretending not to feel, their heart finds room to breathe. Stories lose their power to control us when they are brought into the light. Pain loses its grip when it is shared. And sin, when spoken honestly, begins to loosen its chains.

Yet speaking honestly does not come naturally to most of us. We fear being judged. We fear being misunderstood.

We fear being defined by our worst moments or our deepest wounds. And so, we hold everything inside, hoping no one will notice that we are not as composed as we appear. But while secrecy may protect our image, it does not protect our hearts. Healing requires honesty. Transformation requires truth. And truth begins with recognizing that we are not the only ones who struggle.

In the retreats I lead, participants are invited to write down their wounds on one side of a small purple paper. On the other side of that paper, I ask them to write down their most frequently recurring sin. These papers are not shared. I tell them to put them in their pocket or purse. Near the end of the retreat, I ask everyone to look around the room. Each attendee has a small piece of purple paper listing their hidden wounds and brokenness. People begin to see that they are sitting in what I call a "sea of purple." It is a simple image, yet it carries a profound message: you are not alone. Every person in the room carries something. Every heart has cracks. Every journey has places of darkness. We may not see those places in each other on a Sunday morning, but that does not mean they are not there.

When Jesus gathered with His disciples on the night of the Last Supper, He revealed a pattern that speaks to the heart of every believer. He took bread, blessed it, broke it, and shared it. Those four movements hold a deep and quiet truth about what God desires to do in each of our lives. He chooses us, blesses us, meets us in our brokenness and woundedness, and then shares us with the world so that others may discover the hope we have found.

This pattern does not begin with perfection. It begins with honesty. It begins with recognizing that the stories we hide may be the very stories God wants to use. It begins with understanding that the Christian life is not about pretending we are fine but about discovering the grace that meets us when we are not.

As we journey through this book together, we will look more closely at this pattern Jesus revealed, not simply as a memory from Scripture but as a roadmap for our lives today. You may find yourself in one part of the pattern more than another. You may recognize moments of blessing mixed with places of brokenness. You may discover wounds you haven't acknowledged in years. Wherever you find yourself, you are not alone. God has chosen you; God has blessed you, and God desires to bring healing and purpose into the very places you have kept hidden.

Being at the table was never the end of the story. It was an invitation. An invitation to see ourselves as God sees us, to receive His mercy, and to allow our lives — even the parts we wish were different — to be shared for the good of others.

The journey begins here, with the simple truth that everyone carries something, even the people who look just fine.

CHAPTER TWO

Chosen: God's First Word Over Your Life

Most of us don't go through our days feeling particularly chosen. We feel ordinary, unnoticed at times, and even replaceable. We carry insecurities about our usefulness, our worth, or our gifts. We may wonder whether God is pleased with us or whether He looks at our lives with a mixture of disappointment and patience. In moments of struggle, we sometimes assume that God is busy working through other people — stronger people, holier people, people with fewer cracks in their story — while we stand on the sidelines, waiting to be fixed.

Yet when Jesus gathered with His disciples at the Last Supper, the very first movement of that sacred moment was simple: He took the bread. Before He blessed it, before He broke it, before He shared it, He took it into His hands. In other words, He chose it. In choosing it, He gave it purpose. In His hands, something ordinary became something meaningful. And in the same way, long before we ever understand our purpose or recognize our worth, God chooses us.

This truth appears again and again throughout the Gospels. When Jesus first called His disciples, none of them were auditioning for a role. They were fishermen, tax collectors, ordinary people following ordinary routines. But Jesus saw them differently. He saw through their fears and past failures. He saw beyond their limitations. He called them anyway. "Follow me," He said, not because they were ready, but because He was ready to shape their lives into something extraordinary.

One of the most tender moments in Scripture takes place when Jesus calls Zacchaeus by name. Zacchaeus had climbed a tree, hoping only for a glimpse. He didn't expect Jesus to notice him. He certainly didn't expect Jesus to call him down in front of the crowd. But that's what Jesus did. "Zacchaeus," He said, "come down immediately. I must stay at your house today." Jesus chose him before Zacchaeus apologized for anything, before he promised to change, before he repaired a single wrong. Choosing came first.

We see this pattern in the way Jesus interacted with people everywhere He went. He chose Peter, knowing Peter would one day deny Him. He chose Matthew, knowing Matthew's past made him unpopular with nearly everyone. He chose Mary Magdalene, though others saw her only through the lens of her past. Jesus didn't wait for them to earn His affection. He chose them because that is where transformation begins. Choosing is God's first word over a person's life.

If we pause and let that truth sink in, it can reshape the way we see ourselves. Some believers live with the quiet suspicion that God must be disappointed in them. They replay their mistakes in their minds and wonder if those failures disqualify them from being used by God. They assume that once they become more consistent, more obedient, and more spiritually mature, then God might have a plan for them. But Scripture tells a different story. God's choosing is not delayed until we have everything figured out. It begins right in the middle of our ordinary, imperfect, unpredictable lives.

When Jesus looked across the synagogue one Sabbath and saw a man with a withered hand, He didn't turn away. He called the man forward. When a woman who had been suffering for twelve years reached out to touch the hem of His garment, Jesus stopped, turned, and chose to engage her heart. When a group of friends lowered a paralyzed man through the roof, Jesus chose him before the man could even speak. Choosing always comes before changing.

Yet many believers struggle to accept this. It is one thing to believe that God chooses people in general. It is another thing entirely to believe He chose you. That He knows your name. That He sees your story. That He understands your wounds and failures and still says, "You are mine." Sometimes our own self-doubt speaks louder than God's reassurance. Sometimes the echoes of past criticism drown out the quiet truth that God delights in us, not because we are perfect but because we are His.

Perhaps this is why Jesus spoke so often about sheep. Sheep don't choose their shepherd; the shepherd chooses them. Sheep don't earn affection; they receive it. The shepherd knows each one individually. He knows the limping ones, the stubborn ones, the frightened ones, and the ones who wander off. And He goes after them not because they impress Him, but because they belong to Him. "My sheep hear my voice," Jesus said, "and I know them." He did not say, "I know the best of them." He said, "I know them."

When God chooses us, it is not a temporary assignment or a polite gesture. It is a declaration of belonging. It is the moment in which God says, "Your story is not an accident. Your life is not a mistake. I have called you by name. You are mine." Even when we struggle, even when we fail, even when we hesitate to share our lives with others, God's choosing remains steady. It is the foundation upon which everything else is built.

Many Christians wrestle with this truth. Some are quick to name their failures. Others feel unworthy of being used by God. But something changes when a person begins to believe that God chose them deliberately — not reluctantly, not out of pity, not because no one else was available. When the truth of His choosing takes root, the heart begins to open. Confidence grows. Wounds loosen their grip. People start to see their lives not through the lens of their brokenness but through the eyes of the God who called them.

Being chosen does not mean God overlooks our brokenness. It means He sees it clearly and still calls us anyway. Being chosen does not mean we escape the wounds of life. It means God meets us in those wounds with love that refuses to let go. Being chosen is not a reward for righteousness; it is an invitation into grace.

If we could look at our lives the way God does, we might be surprised by what He sees. We might see the potential hidden beneath our fear. We might notice the compassion that grew from our wounds or the strength that emerged from our trials. We might recognize the quiet ways God has used us without our knowing it. God's choosing is not limited by our past or our present struggles. It is rooted in His love, and His love has a purpose.

The journey of faith begins not with our effort but with God's initiative. Before we learn to bless others, God blesses us. Before we face our brokenness, God assures us of His mercy. Before we are shared with the world, we are held in His hands. Everything starts with being chosen.

As you continue reading, you may begin noticing moments in your own life when God reached for you, moments you did not recognize as His choosing at the time. They may be small, gentle moments — a conversation, a nudge, a whisper — or they may be unmistakable turning points. Either way, they are reminders that God has been writing your story with intention from the very beginning.

You are chosen.

Not by accident.

Not reluctantly.

Not because no one else was available.

You are chosen because God sees in you what you cannot yet see in yourself.

And choosing is only the beginning.

CHAPTER THREE
Blessed: The Gift We Forget to Notice

When Jesus took the bread at the Last Supper, His next movement was simple: He blessed it. He lifted it, gave thanks, and acknowledged the Father's goodness. In that moment, nothing outwardly changed about the bread. It looked the same. It felt the same. But something had shifted. It had been spoken over. It had been blessed.

The same is true in our lives. After God chooses us, He blesses us — often in ways we do not immediately recognize. Sometimes His blessing is as clear as an answered prayer or a surprising provision. Other times it is quieter, woven into our days so gently that we only notice it when we stop long enough to look back. But whether we see it or not, blessing is always God's next word over a chosen life.

Many Christians struggle to believe this. They know they are supposed to feel blessed. They know they should be grateful. But life has not always turned out the way they imagined. When blessings seem thin and trials seem thick, the word "blessed" can feel distant or unreachable. Some look at their lives and see mostly the things that went wrong — the prayers that went unanswered, the dreams that did not unfold, the wounds they still carry. Others compare themselves to people who appear more fortunate and quietly conclude they must have slipped through God's fingers when blessings were handed out.

But blessing is rarely measured by circumstances alone. It is something deeper, something steadier, something rooted not in what is happening around us, but in what God is doing within us. Blessing does not always remove difficulties, but it gives us the strength to face them. It does not guarantee a smooth path, but it assures us we will not walk the path alone. Blessing is God's way of saying, "I am with you, and my goodness will meet you in every place your feet will go."

One day, Jesus was teaching on a hillside when He spoke words that surprised everyone listening. "Blessed are the poor in spirit," He said. "Blessed are those who mourn. Blessed are the meek." He went on to describe situations that no one in the crowd would have described as blessed — hunger, grief, persecution, need. Yet Jesus called these people blessed not because their circumstances were easy, but because God was near to them in ways they could not yet see. The blessing was not in the struggle; it was in God's presence at the heart of the struggle.

This tells us something important: blessing and difficulty are not opposites. They often appear side by side in the very same story. A person may walk through grief and still find themselves carried by peace they cannot explain. Another may fight a recurring sin but discover that God's mercy meets them every time they fall. Someone else may endure a season of loneliness only to realize later that God was preparing them for a friendship they would have missed had life gone any other way. Blessings often appear in ways that do not announce themselves. It is quiet, steady, and patient in ways we often overlook.

Sometimes blessing looks like protection. Sometimes it looks like restoration. Sometimes it looks like conviction — the gentle nudge that keeps us from wandering too far from the path God desires. And sometimes blessing looks like mercy, especially in the places where we least expect it. It's the moment we receive forgiveness instead of the judgment we feared. It's the kindness that finds us after a mistake. It's the love that remains even when we feel unlovable.

Mercy is one of God's greatest blessings, yet we often forget to notice it. We remember our failures quickly. We remember our regrets. We remember the times we promised God we would do better, only to find ourselves repeating the same patterns. But what we often overlook is how God keeps meeting us with mercy anyway. He blesses us with another chance. He blesses us with patience. He blesses us with grace that outlasts our weakness.

If we were to trace the blessings of our lives — not just the obvious ones but the hidden ones — we might be amazed by what we find. We might notice how a season that felt empty later produced wisdom we needed. We might see how a disappointment redirected us toward something better. We might realize how a person who seemed difficult to love taught us compassion we didn't know we lacked. Blessings are not always wrapped in bright paper. Sometimes they come disguised as challenges, detours, lessons, or slow-growing strength.

In my ministry, I've often met people who underestimate the blessings God has already placed in them. They look at their lives and see only flaws. They see the temper they wish they didn't have, the fear that keeps resurfacing, the habit they are ashamed of. But if you gently ask them about their lives, a different picture emerges. They may not notice it, but others do. You begin to see patience that grew through hardship, courage that formed through loss, or compassion that blossomed from surviving something difficult. These are blessings, even if we didn't ask for them and even if we would never have chosen the path that produced them.

Jesus blessed the bread before He broke it. That simple detail holds a truth many of us overlook. We are blessed before we recognize our brokenness. We are blessed even when we feel fragile. We are blessed before we are fully healed. Blessing does not wait for perfection. It rests on our lives because God is good, not because we are flawless.

When we begin to see ourselves as blessed — not because our lives are easy, but because God is near — something inside us softens. We become more patient with others. We become more grateful. We become less afraid of facing our brokenness because we know it is cradled in the hands of a God who has already spoken blessing over us.

Imagine what might change if we viewed our lives through the lens of blessing instead of shortage. We might stop comparing ourselves to others. We might celebrate the gifts God placed uniquely within us. We might become more attentive to His presence in the ordinary moments of our days. And we might discover that our greatest calling is not to achieve something spectacular, but to recognize that we have been blessed so that we can be a blessing to others.

The journey of the Christian life always begins with being chosen, but it cannot grow without understanding that we are blessed. Blessing steadies us. Blessing prepares us. Blessing reminds us that God is not waiting for us to be perfect before He works through us. He has already spoken good over our lives. He has already placed His mercy within reach. He has already looked at who we are — and who we are becoming — and declared that His grace is enough for every step ahead.

As we continue walking through the pattern Jesus revealed, we will soon come face-to-face with the part of the story we often avoid: brokenness and woundedness. But before we turn toward that tender place, pause for a moment and let this truth settle gently in your heart.

You are blessed.

Right now.

Right where you are.

Long before anything changes.

Long before your story feels complete.

Blessed because God is with you.

Blessed because His mercy is upon you.

Blessed because His love does not depend on your perfection.

God's blessing is His way of saying, "You are not alone. I am with you. And my goodness will meet you in every place you go."

And that blessing is what prepares us for everything that comes next.

CHAPTER FOUR

Broken and Wounded:
Where Grace Meets the Truth About Us

By the time Jesus blessed the bread at the Last Supper, something sacred had already taken place. He had chosen it. He had spoken good over it. And then came the movement most of us would rather skip: Jesus broke it. For many believers, this is the part of the pattern we understand least. We prefer the choosing. We appreciate the blessing. But the breaking feels difficult, uncomfortable, and sometimes frightening. Yet this is the place where God often does His deepest work. It is where grace meets truth and begins transforming us from the inside out.

When we talk about brokenness, we usually think of the mistakes we make, the temptations that pull at us, and the habits we wish we could shake. These are the places where we recognize our part in the story, where we see clearly that our own decisions have led us down paths we regret. Brokenness grows from the sin we commit, the words we wish we could take back, the actions we knew better than to take, and the choices that leave us wondering why we keep falling into the same patterns. This kind of brokenness is familiar to all of us, even if we struggle to admit it. It is the place where we say, "Lord, I did this," and hope He will meet us with forgiveness.

But brokenness is only half the story. The other half is woundedness, and it carries a different kind of weight. Woundedness comes from the things we did not choose, the moments that found us without our asking, the hurts that entered our lives through the hands or decisions of others. These wounds can be sharp and sudden — like the loss of a child, a tragic accident, an unexpected diagnosis, or the death of a spouse after decades of shared life. Or they can be slow and lingering — like neglect, rejection, strained relationships, or the subtle ache of hopes that have quietly faded over time.

Wounds are not our fault, yet they shape us deeply. They settle into our hearts and memories in ways we do not always understand. And often, the deeper the wound, the harder it becomes to put into words. Grief has a way of quieting us. Trauma teaches us to hide. Heartache convinces us that if we speak too freely, the pain will spill out in ways we cannot contain. Many people who appear steady and calm on the outside are holding far more inside than anyone realizes.

This is why the breaking movement of Jesus is so profound. When He took the bread and broke it, He was revealing a truth about Himself — and about us. Breaking does not happen because something is worthless. Breaking happens because what is broken is about to be shared. Jesus was preparing to pour Himself out for the world. His breaking was not a sign of weakness; it was the doorway through which His love would flow.

In the same way, our brokenness and woundedness are not the end of our stories. They are the places where God meets us with compassion and begins to write something new. But we cannot receive that grace as long as everything remains hidden. Brokenness kept in silence grows heavier with time. Wounds left unspoken take root and deepen. And the more we try to handle everything ourselves, the more we convince ourselves that no one would understand — that our struggles are too shameful, or our wounds too personal, or our failures too repeated to ever be lifted into the light.

Yet the truth is far different. The struggles we hide are often the struggles others share. The wounds we think no one sees are present in more people than we realize. The sins we confess privately over and over again, hoping this time will be the last, are the very places where countless believers quietly battle the same patterns. I have met people who feel hopeless because they have confessed the same sin a thousand times to God but have never spoken it aloud to a single person. They wonder why nothing changes. They wonder why transformation feels out of reach. What they do not realize is that secrecy has become its own burden, its own chain.

Grace is always available, but it often waits for us to make room for it. And honesty is what creates that room. When we acknowledge our brokenness, we are not telling

God something He does not already know. We are simply agreeing with Him about the truth of our hearts. When we name our wounds, we are not reopening them — we are giving God access to the places that need His healing touch. When we speak openly with another trusted believer, we are loosening the grip that shame has held on us for years.

Grace meets us in the truth, not in the pretending. Grace moves toward the honest heart, not the polished one. God does not expect us to be unbroken or unwounded before coming to Him. He invites us to bring the whole story — the sin we regret, the pain we carry, the questions we have never voiced, and the moments we wish had never happened. Nothing in our life surprises Him. Nothing frightens Him away. Nothing makes Him reconsider His choosing or withdraw His blessing.

Some people avoid facing their brokenness because they fear what they will find. Others avoid acknowledging their wounds because they do not want to relive the memories they buried long ago. But God does not lead us into these places to condemn us or overwhelm us. He leads us there gently, lovingly, so that we can discover what He has known all along: our broken places are not barriers to Him. They are the places where His mercy holds us most closely.

When we begin to speak honestly about these parts of our story, something remarkable happens. Our brokenness becomes a place of connection, not isolation. Our wounds become bridges of compassion. The very moments we thought disqualified us become the moments God uses to help others feel understood. When someone shares a struggle they have carried in silence, and another person says, "I've been there too," the weight begins to lift. When someone sheds tears for a loss they have never put into words, and someone else listens with patience and love, healing quietly begins.

I have seen this time and time again in retreats, small groups, church gatherings, and in the simple conversations that unfold when people finally feel safe enough to speak. No one wants to be defined by their brokenness or their wounds. But when we hide those places, we miss the opportunity to experience the grace God offers through honesty and community. And we miss the chance to become part of someone else's healing story.

Brokenness and woundedness are not obstacles to God's work in our lives. They are the places where His love takes root most deeply. They remind us that we are human, that we need one another, and that we depend on a God who meets us exactly where we are. When we bring these places into the light, we discover that God has never turned away from them. He has been waiting for us to let Him in.

If you are carrying a broken place in your life, know this: God sees it clearly and loves you entirely. If you are holding a wound you never asked for, remember this: God is near to the brokenhearted and binds up their wounds. If you feel ashamed of the patterns you cannot seem to break, hear the truth in your heart — God's mercy is new every morning, and His grace is strong enough for your weakness.

As we continue walking through the pattern Jesus revealed, we will soon arrive at the movement that surprises many people — the moment when brokenness becomes a blessing not only to us but to others. But first, pause for a moment and let this truth settle gently:

Your brokenness does not disqualify you.

Your woundedness does not diminish you.

God meets you in both.

And He never lets go of what He intends to heal.

CHAPTER FIVE

Shared: The Gift God Gives Through Our Lives

When Jesus broke the bread at the Last Supper, He did not set the pieces aside. He did not hold them for Himself or place them back on the table. He gave them away. He shared them with the people He loved. The choosing had meaning. The blessing had meaning. The breaking had meaning. But it was the sharing that revealed the purpose of the whole pattern.

In the same way, God does not choose us only for our comfort or bless us only for our personal encouragement. He does not meet us in our brokenness and woundedness simply so we can feel better about ourselves. Each movement has a purpose, and that purpose becomes clear when God leads us outward — into the lives of others. A Christian life that ends with only self-reflection, only private prayer, only inward growth, is like bread that is chosen, blessed, and broken but never given. The story is incomplete.

Sharing is the movement most Christians long for but

also fear. We want our lives to matter. We want to make a difference. We want others to know God is real and active. Yet many believers hesitate to share their stories, their faith, or their experiences. They feel unworthy. They feel inexperienced. They fear saying the wrong thing or looking foolish. And for many, the greatest barrier of all is the quiet belief that their story is too broken, too wounded, too ordinary to help anyone else.

But throughout the Gospels, we see Jesus choosing ordinary, imperfect people to carry extraordinary hope into the world. When He healed the man who had been tormented by evil spirits, He told him, "Go home to your people and tell them how much the Lord has done for you." When He spoke with the woman at the well, she left her water jar and ran to tell her community what had happened. When He raised Lazarus from the dead, many came to believe simply because others shared what they had witnessed.

God has always used everyday stories to awaken faith in the hearts of others. Not grand speeches. Not perfect testimonies. Not flawless lives. Just honest stories told by honest people who have experienced God's mercy in the places where they once felt alone.

This is the beauty of the shared life — it does not require us to be experts, scholars, or polished communicators. It requires something far simpler and far more powerful: authenticity. When a believer speaks with humility and honesty about the ways God has carried them, comforted them, forgiven them, strengthened them, or met them in a time of need, something opens in the heart of the listener. Walls come down. Hope rises. And people begin to realize that if God met someone else in their brokenness, maybe He will meet them in theirs.

Yet sharing is not only about speaking. It is also about presence. It is about showing up for others with compassion, patience, and love. It is about listening without judgment. It is about noticing the people who sit beside us in church week after week — the ones carrying pain we never ask about, the ones smiling on the outside while wondering if anyone sees their struggle. We often assume everyone around us is doing fine. But if we could see the invisible stories in the hearts of the people nearest to us — in front of us, behind us, beside us — we would realize how many are quietly hurting, longing for someone who cares enough to ask, "How are you really doing?"

When we share ourselves with others, we become the instruments God uses to bring hope and healing. We do not heal them — only God does that. But He often chooses to work through the kindness, empathy, and honesty of His people. A comforting word. A listening ear. A story shared at the right moment. A prayer whispered when someone feels too weary to pray for themselves. These simple acts carry more power than we realize.

Sharing is also where our own healing deepens. Something happens in the human heart when we step out of secrecy and into connection. Shame loses its grip. Fear loosens. The burden feels lighter. When I began sharing my own story after years of holding it inside, I discovered something unexpected — my story wasn't just for me. As others heard it, something in them opened too. They felt permission to speak. They felt safe to be honest. They felt less alone. What I had kept hidden for so long became the very thing God used to help others begin their own journey toward healing.

This is why sharing matters. Not because we want to put our wounds on display, and certainly not because we seek attention. Sharing matters because our honesty becomes someone else's lifeline. When we speak the truth of our lives, we create a space where others can speak theirs. When we reveal the parts of our story touched by God's mercy, we help others believe His mercy can reach them too.

But sharing is not only about our brokenness and woundedness. It is also about sharing our blessings — the insights God has given us, the compassion He has grown in us, the lessons learned through difficult seasons. When you have walked through grief, you become a source of comfort for someone who is grieving. When you have struggled with a recurring sin, you become a voice of understanding for someone fighting the same battle. When you have survived a loss you thought would undo you, you become a witness to the power of God's sustaining grace.

Many believers underestimate how important their presence is in the lives of others. They assume someone else is better equipped, more knowledgeable, or more spiritually mature. But the truth is simple: God places people in our path for a reason. There are conversations only you can have. There are individuals who will listen to your story in a way they might not listen to someone else's. God weaves your experiences, your personality, your wounds, and your blessings together into a story that becomes a gift to those around you.

The shared life is not about having all the answers. It is about offering what we have — our time, our attention, our compassion, and our story — trusting that God will use it in ways we may never fully see. Some of the greatest impacts you will ever make will happen quietly, in moments that seem small. A gentle encouragement at the right time. A hand on the shoulder of someone who feels unnoticed. A simple statement like, "You're not alone." These are the moments when God's love becomes visible through us.

As Jesus shared the bread with His disciples, He was revealing something essential about the nature of God's kingdom: it grows through generosity. It spreads through openness. It moves from heart to heart through people who are willing to give of themselves. A faith that remains private, hidden, or unspoken cannot nourish anyone — not even the one who holds it. But a faith shared becomes a source of life for everyone it touches.

Sharing is where the choosing, blessing, and breaking find their purpose. It is the moment when God takes everything we have lived — the beautiful and the painful, the joyful and the difficult — and turns it outward toward the healing of others. It is where our lives begin to ripple outward, touching the stories around us in ways we may never fully understand.

If you long for your life to matter in the kingdom of God, remember this: it already does. The question is not whether God can use you. He has been preparing you from the beginning. The question is whether you are willing to let your life be shared — gently, honestly, and generously — so that others can discover the hope God placed within you.

You have been chosen.

You have been blessed.

You have experienced the reality of brokenness and the comfort of grace.

And now, God invites you into the final movement of the pattern:

Your life is a gift — meant to be shared.

CHAPTER SIX

Living the Pattern: When the Table Becomes a Way of Life

Most Christians know the story of the Lord's Supper. They have heard the words, pictured the scene, and felt its sacred weight. But far fewer recognize that Jesus wasn't only giving His disciples something to remember. He was giving them a pattern to live — a way of understanding their identity, their purpose, and their calling.

Chosen.

Blessed.

Broken.

Shared.

These four movements were not meant to stay on the pages of Scripture. They were meant to be written into our lives. The table was the beginning, not the end. Jesus never intended His followers to simply recall what happened in the upper room. He intended them to carry it with them, to let it shape how they saw themselves, how they saw others, and how they stepped into the world.

For many believers, the idea of "living the pattern" feels abstract until they realize it is far simpler — and far more personal — than they expected. The pattern unfolds slowly, almost quietly, in the everyday moments of our lives. It shapes our thoughts, our choices, our relationships, and the ways we respond to both joy and hardship. It becomes a way of seeing the world not through our fears or insecurities, but through the tenderness of God's grace.

When we remember we are chosen, something begins to shift internally. The question is no longer, *"Does my life matter?"* but *"How is God choosing to work through me today?"* This awareness softens the heart. It steadies the mind. It replaces insecurity with a quiet courage that comes from knowing our story has a purpose. When a believer knows they are chosen, they stop waiting for someone else to live the Christian life for them. They begin awakening to the truth that God has already written them into His story.

When we recognize that we are blessed, we become more open to noticing God's presence in the daily rhythms of life. Gratitude becomes easier. Fear loosens its grip. We begin to see not only the good things God has given us, but also the ways He has sustained us through the difficult things we did not choose. The blessing movement helps us realize we are not walking alone. It teaches us to trust that God is working even in seasons that feel unfinished or unclear.

When we acknowledge our brokenness and woundedness, we stop pretending. We stop performing.

We stop wearing the mask that tells the world everything is fine when our hearts are carrying far more than we admit. And in that honesty, we experience something powerful: God meets us where we are. Grace becomes real. Healing begins. This is the place where the Christian life becomes authentic — not polished or perfect but anchored in mercy.

And when we allow our lives to be shared, something beautiful unfolds. The purpose of the pattern finally comes into view. The choosing wasn't only for us. The blessing wasn't only to comfort us. The healing wasn't only to restore us. All of it was preparing us to become instruments of hope in the lives of others. When we share our lives with gentleness and grace, God uses our stories — our real, imperfect, deeply human stories — to touch hearts and awaken faith.

Living this pattern does not require dramatic moments or grand gestures. It simply asks us to be attentive, open, and willing.

We live the pattern when we listen patiently to someone who is hurting.

We live the pattern when we forgive someone who wounded us deeply.

We live the pattern when we admit we are struggling and ask for help.

We live the pattern when we pray for someone by name.

We live the pattern when we encourage a friend who feels unseen.

We live the pattern when we choose compassion over criticism.

We live the pattern when we let God use our lives, not despite our brokenness, but through it.

Sometimes living the pattern means stepping into a conversation that feels awkward or vulnerable. Sometimes it means offering kindness when we would rather turn inward. Sometimes it means giving someone the gift of our time when our schedules feel full. And sometimes it means having the courage to share a part of our story we've kept hidden for too long.

The pattern becomes a way of life not through one dramatic decision, but through a thousand small choices, made faithfully, day after day.

Over the years, I have watched people come alive when they begin practicing this rhythm. It's as if a light begins to grow inside them — not a spotlight, but the steady glow of someone who understands why their life matters. They become less weighed down by their past. They become more attentive to the needs of others. They become gracious with themselves and compassionate toward the people around them. They begin to see that God is weaving their story into something far more meaningful than they imagined.

What surprises many believers is how natural this pattern becomes once they start paying attention. They notice God's choosing in ordinary moments — in a conversation, a decision, or a gentle prompting. They recognize His blessings not only in answered prayers but in the strength that carried them through hard days. They face their brokenness with honesty, knowing they are held by a love that does not fail. And they share their lives with greater freedom, trusting that God will use even their smallest acts of kindness for His purposes.

Living the pattern is not about striving or trying harder. It is about becoming aware of what God is already doing and responding with openness. It is about letting the love that touched us move through us. It is about surrendering the fear that tells us we have nothing to offer. It is about stepping into each day with a willingness to be used for good.

As we continue this journey, you may begin to see the pattern everywhere—not because you are forcing it, but because it is written into the very heart of the Christian life. It is how God shapes us. It is how He strengthens us. It is how He sends us into a world longing for authenticity, hope, and grace.

Being at the table was just the beginning.

The real story is the life we live afterward.

CHAPTER SEVEN
A Community of the Shared Life

When we think of Christian community, we often picture people gathered together — worshiping, praying, singing, serving. These are beautiful expressions of faith, but community is deeper than activities. True Christian community is formed when people share their lives with one another, not just their schedules. It grows when believers become honest, attentive, and compassionate toward the hearts of those around them.

The pattern Jesus revealed — chosen, blessed, broken, shared — is not only a pattern for individual believers. It is a pattern for the entire body of Christ. When a group of people begins living this pattern together, something remarkable happens. The church becomes more than a place to attend; it becomes a family to belong to. The people sitting in the pew in front of us, behind us, and beside us are no longer strangers. They become fellow travelers on a sacred journey.

Yet many churches struggle to reach this depth of community because most Christians do not feel safe being honest. They show up each week carrying their wounds, their worries, their failures, and their private battles — but they smile, shake hands, and quietly return to their seats without ever letting anyone see what is really happening inside them. The fear of appearing weak or flawed keeps them silent. The belief that "everyone else has it together" convinces them they are the only ones struggling. And so, the church becomes a gathering of people who appear fine but feel alone.

This is where the pattern changes everything. When a church understands that every person is both broken and blessed, both wounded and chosen, something inside the community shifts. Compassion begins to replace judgment. Understanding replaces assumptions. Patience replaces impatience. People stop expecting perfection from themselves and from others. Instead, they begin creating a space where honesty is welcomed, and burdens are shared.

Imagine a church where people enter knowing they do not have to pretend — where a struggling parent can admit they feel overwhelmed, where a grieving widower can say they are lonely, where a teenager can confess they feel lost, and where someone battling a secret sin can finally speak the truth without fear of shame. These are the communities where true healing happens. These are the communities where people encounter not only the teachings of Jesus but also His compassion.

This kind of community does not appear instantly. It grows slowly, quietly, one honest conversation at a time. It begins when one person chooses to be real. It deepens when someone else realizes they are not alone. It takes root when people listen more than they advise, care more than they judge, and love more than they analyze.

Shared lives create shared strength.

A community like this recognizes that every person carries a story, even the ones who appear confident and unshaken. The couple sitting two rows over may be carrying a fear they have not voiced. The man who volunteers every week may be struggling with a recurring sin that weighs heavily on him. The woman who greets everyone with a smile may be grieving something she has never spoken aloud. The teenager who sits quietly may be longing for someone who sees them. When we begin to look at the people around us through this lens, our hearts become gentler, and our words become kinder.

A shared life also means allowing others to help us carry what is too heavy for us alone. This does not require dramatic confessions or long explanations. Sometimes it is as simple as telling someone, "I've had a difficult week," or "I'm walking through something hard right now." Other times it means letting someone pray for us, letting someone listen, or opening up enough to say, "I could use a friend today." These small moments of vulnerability become doorways through which God's grace enters our lives.

Over the years, I have seen countless Christians discover healing not only in the prayers they offer but also in the people who walk beside them. Support groups, Bible studies, friendship groups, and fellowship gatherings become places where believers begin to see themselves not as isolated individuals but as part of a living, breathing community held together by God's love. When a community begins to live the shared life, no one is left to struggle alone.

The shared life also changes how we serve. Instead of volunteering out of obligation, we begin serving out of gratitude. Instead of trying to fix others, we learn to walk with them. Instead of assuming we are the strong ones helping the weak, we realize we all need one another. Service becomes less about tasks and more about relationships. It becomes less about doing something for someone and more about being present with them.

What surprises many believers is how deeply people respond when they feel genuinely cared for. A listening ear can bring someone hope. A gentle question can open a closed heart. A simple act of kindness can remind someone they matter. Sharing our lives with others creates a ripple effect that moves far beyond anything we might see in the moment.

A church living this pattern does not need to be large, polished, or impressive. It needs to be real. Real love. Real conversations. Real support. Real grace. These are the ingredients that make a church feel like home.

As this book continues to unfold, you may find yourself

thinking of people in your life who could use someone who cares. You might begin noticing the quiet needs behind someone's smile. You might sense God nudging you toward someone who seems distant or discouraged. When you feel those nudges, pay attention. They may be the beginning of God using your life — your chosen, blessed, broken, and shared life — to touch someone else's story.

The community of shared life is not built by programs or committees. It is built by people who are willing to show up as they are and care for others as they are. It is built by people who recognize that the gospel is not just a message to be preached but a love to be lived. And it is built by people who understand that Jesus did not simply give bread to His disciples — He gave Himself.

When we share our lives with others, we follow in His footsteps. We are allowing His love to move through our hands, our words, and our presence. We are becoming the answer to someone else's prayer. And in doing so, we discover that community was God's gift to us all along — a place where we can be honest, supported, encouraged, and loved.

The shared life is not a burden.

It is a blessing.

It is where faith becomes tangible.

It is where love becomes real.

It is where the pattern becomes alive.

CHAPTER EIGHT

Sent Into the World: Where the Pattern Touches Everyday Life

When Jesus shared the bread among His disciples, He wasn't simply giving them something to eat. He was giving them a mission. The table was a beginning, a starting point for a life that would take them far beyond the walls of the upper room. In the same way, the pattern of chosen, blessed, broken, and shared does not end in Christian community. It moves outward into the world where real people live real lives with real struggles.

Every time we walk out the doors of a church, we are stepping into the very place where Jesus sends us to live what we have received. We carry the pattern into grocery stores, office buildings, neighborhoods, workplaces, classrooms, waiting rooms, and family gatherings. We carry it into the lives of friends and strangers, into ordinary conversations and unexpected moments. The pattern becomes a way of seeing every encounter as an opportunity for God to work through us.

Many Christians underestimate how profoundly their everyday lives can touch others. We imagine that kingdom work must be dramatic or visible — preaching, teaching, leading, organizing. Yet Jesus spent much of His ministry in simple, ordinary moments with ordinary people. He talked by the wells. He walked dusty roads. He ate meals with people who never expected a rabbi to sit at their table. He noticed the overlooked, the lonely, the hurting, and the confused. He brought compassion to places that did not look sacred, and in doing so, He revealed that God's love belongs everywhere.

We live the pattern when we take this same posture into the world. When we step out of our front door with the quiet intention to see others the way Jesus sees them, the pattern becomes active. We begin to notice people we might have overlooked. We begin to listen more carefully. We begin to slow down long enough to pay attention to the person in front of us, realizing that God may be at work in ways we cannot see.

Living a shared life in the world does not require grand gestures. Most of the time, it looks like gentleness in moments that could have turned sharp. It looks like patience when stress is high. It looks like kindness given freely. It looks like being present in conversations instead of rushing past them. It looks like offering hope where discouragement has taken root. These small, almost invisible moments often touch hearts more deeply than we realize.

You may never know the full impact of a simple conversation, a compassionate word, or a listening ear. But God knows. He sees every act of love, no matter how small. And He often uses the smallest moments to open the largest doors.

Think for a moment about the people you encounter in the course of a week. The coworker who seems distant. The neighbor who rarely speaks. The cashier who appears tired. The friend who puts on a brave face but carries something heavy behind their smile. The stranger sitting alone. Every one of these people carries a story. Some are walking through heartache. Some are fighting battles no one knows about. Some are longing for reassurance that their life matters. And some are praying silently for someone to notice them.

We rarely know the full depth of someone's pain. But we can bring the presence of Christ into their day simply by showing up with sincerity and kindness. When we live the pattern outwardly, we become people who approach others with openness. We stop assuming we understand their circumstances and begin offering them the same grace God has offered us.

Living a shared life also changes how we view our own purpose. Instead of seeing our days as random or routine, we begin to sense that God is weaving meaning into the moments we once overlooked. That conversation you had was not accidental. That interaction with a stranger was not without purpose. That small act of kindness may have been exactly what someone needed to keep going. Our lives become fuller, more intentional, more aligned with God's heart for the world.

Some people feel uncertain about their ability to share their lives with others outside the church. They fear saying the wrong thing or not knowing enough. But the shared life does not begin with speaking — it begins with noticing. It begins with caring. It begins with being willing. God often opens the door when He is ready. Our part is simply to walk through it when it appears.

Sometimes sharing means telling a part of your story when someone needs to hear that they are not alone. Sometimes it means offering encouragement to someone who is struggling. Sometimes it means praying silently for someone you sense is hurting. And sometimes it means showing kindness to someone without expecting anything in return. These small choices can ripple outward in ways we may never fully understand.

What many believers discover is that living the pattern in the world brings unexpected joy. When we let God use our lives to bless others, even in small ways, something awakens in us. We feel connected to His heart. We feel aligned with His purpose. We feel the quiet satisfaction that comes from knowing our life made someone else's day a little lighter. This is not about drawing attention to ourselves. It is about letting God's love shine through the cracks and corners of our lives.

The shared life is also a continual reminder that we are not only sent into the world — we are sent with God. He does not ask us to carry His presence alone. He walks with us. He guides our thoughts. He gives us words when we need them. He opens doors we could not open ourselves. The pattern is not something we try to live through our own strength; it is something God empowers us to live through His grace.

One of the beautiful surprises of living the pattern is how it transforms not only others, but also us. The more we give ourselves away in love, the more we receive. The more we share compassion, the more compassionate we become. The more we listen with sincerity, the more attentive our hearts grow. The more we step into someone else's story, the more clearly we see the purpose God has written into our own.

The shared life is not something we add to our schedule. It is the way we live our schedule. It is the posture we carry into every encounter. It is the quiet awareness that God intends to use our lives — our chosen, blessed, broken, and shared lives — to touch the world He loves.

When we live this pattern daily, we begin to understand why Jesus said, "You are the light of the world." Light is not loud. Light is not forceful. Light does not argue or demand attention. It simply shines. And in shining, it reveals goodness, hope, and the gentle presence of God.

Each day, God invites you into this quiet shining. Into

this sharing. Into this purpose. The table was the beginning, but your life is the continuation.

You are sent into the world, not alone, not empty, not unprepared — but chosen, blessed, broken in honest ways, and shared in love.

CHAPTER NINE
The Fears That Hold Us Back

Most Christians want their lives to make a difference. They want to encourage others, to offer hope, to be a quiet presence of God's love in a hurting world. They want to share their stories in ways that help someone else feel less alone. And yet, even with the best intentions, many believers remain silent. Something inside them hesitates. Something holds them back.

What holds us back is rarely a lack of compassion or willingness. It is almost always fear. Not the loud, dramatic fear of danger, but the quiet, internal fear that whispers to the heart and makes us second-guess our worth, our story, or our readiness.

Some believers hesitate because they don't feel good enough. They see their flaws more clearly than their strengths. They carry memories of failures, promises broken, mistakes repeated. They wonder how God could possibly use them when they still struggle in so many ways. They imagine that sharing their faith or their story requires a level of spiritual maturity they haven't yet reached. And so, they wait, hoping one day they will feel worthy enough to speak.

But God has never waited for perfect people. Jesus called fishermen with unsteady faith. He invited tax collectors with questionable reputations. He welcomed people who made impulsive choices, people who doubted, people who misunderstood Him, people who failed Him. What mattered was not their perfection but their willingness. God still works the same way. He does not ask you to be flawless; He asks you to be open.

Other believers remain silent because of shame. Shame has a way of settling into the deeper parts of our stories, especially in the places marked by sin, regret, or personal failure. Shame tells us that if people really knew us — the whole us, the imperfect us — they would pull away. Shame convinces us that our story is too messy, too embarrassing, too complicated to ever be spoken out loud. And so, we lock those parts of our lives behind closed doors, hoping no one will ever see them.

Yet shame's power grows in the dark. The moment we speak honestly — even to one safe person — something heavy lifts. The fear loses its grip. And we discover that we are not the only ones who have struggled, not the only ones who have fallen, not the only ones who have carried a hidden weight. Honesty does not expose us to rejection; it often opens the door to connection.

Some believers fear rejection. They worry that sharing

will make others uncomfortable or cause someone to withdraw. They worry about saying the wrong thing or revealing too much. And their concerns are not foolish; not every environment is safe, and vulnerability requires wisdom. Sharing our lives does not mean revealing everything to everyone. It means allowing God's light into the places where He prompts us, with people He has prepared to receive our story with care. When we share with discernment, it becomes an act of trust — not only in others but in God's ability to guide our steps.

Then there are those who simply feel inadequate. They look at others who seem stronger, wiser, more articulate. They assume they don't know enough Scripture, don't pray eloquently enough, don't have the right words. But the shared life is not built on eloquence; it is built on sincerity. God uses humble voices far more often than polished ones. People listen not because someone speaks perfectly but because they speak authentically. The most meaningful encouragement you will ever give will likely come from a place of honesty, not expertise.

Some Christians hold back because they worry that sharing will stir up old pain. They have walked through wounds so deep they can barely name them. The thought of speaking them aloud feels overwhelming. But sharing does not mean reliving the hurt. It means allowing God to bring gentle light into the places we once kept hidden. It means letting someone sit beside us in our pain, rather than carrying it alone. And often, it means offering someone else the comfort we once longed for ourselves.

There are also believers who want to share but simply do not know how to begin. They imagine they need a well-formed testimony or a dramatic story. But sharing rarely begins with something grand. It often begins with a small sentence: "I've felt that way too." Or "You're not alone." Or "I understand that kind of struggle." These simple words open hearts. They create a connection. They allow God to enter a conversation with His quiet, healing presence.

When we look closely at all these fears — unworthiness, shame, rejection, inadequacy, fear of old wounds, uncertainty about how to begin — we see a common thread: each assumes that sharing depends on our strength. But it doesn't. It never has. The shared life depends on God's presence, not our perfection.

God does not send us into someone else's story alone. He goes with us. He gives us the words we need at the moment we need them. He prepares hearts in ways we cannot see. He uses even our hesitant steps to accomplish more than we ever imagined.

Fear does not disappear completely, even for seasoned believers. But fear loses its authority when we remember that our lives are not our own — they are vessels for God's love. Every time we take a small step forward, the fear grows quieter. Every time we risk honesty, the fear loosens its grip. Every time we speak gently into someone else's life, the fear is replaced by a sense of purpose.

It may feel frightening to share your life — your blessings, your brokenness, your wounds, your stories — but the very thing you fear may be the thing God uses most. You may never know how deeply your honesty will touch someone. You may never know how your story becomes the turning point in someone else's journey. But God knows. And He invites you to trust Him with the outcome.

Fear may tap you on the shoulder, but it does not have to lead you. God can use your life — exactly as it is — to shine light into someone else's darkness. You are not sharing because you are perfect. You are sharing because God's grace is.

CHAPTER TEN
A Life That Leaves a Mark

When Jesus shared the bread at the Last Supper, He wasn't only offering nourishment to His disciples. He was showing them the kind of life He intended them to live — a life poured out for others, a life given away in love. The sharing of the bread was more than a moment; it was an invitation. It was His way of saying, "This is how you change the world. Not by holding your life tightly, but by giving it generously."

Every believer carries the desire to leave something meaningful behind. We want our lives to matter. We hope that something we say, or do, or offer will outlast us. And yet, most of us doubt that anything we do has lasting value. We imagine that legacies belong to people with impressive gifts, large platforms, or extraordinary stories. But God sees legacies differently. In His hands, even the smallest act of love becomes a seed that grows in ways we may never see.

A legacy rarely looks dramatic while it is being formed. It takes shape quietly, almost invisibly, in the gentle ways we offer ourselves to others. A kind word spoken at the right moment. A listening ear extended when someone feels alone. A conversation that helps someone breathe a little easier. These moments may seem small to us, but they can become life-changing to the person who receives them.

People don't always remember the details of what we say, but they remember how we made them feel. They remember who paused long enough to care. They remember who looked them in the eye when they felt invisible. They remember who walked with them through difficult seasons. These simple, steady choices carve a mark into the heart that does not fade.

Our honesty also leaves a mark. When we allow others to see the parts of our story that aren't polished or perfect, we give them permission to be honest with their own. We show them that faith isn't a performance but a journey. We show them that God works in real lives — not ideal ones. And in that honesty, we become bridges for others to cross into their own healing. The parts of our story we once wished we could hide often become the very places where others find hope.

Courage leaves a mark as well. Not the kind of courage that stands on a stage, but the quiet courage that chooses compassion when it would be easier to turn away. The courage that reaches out instead of shrinking back. The courage that speaks up when someone else needs a voice. The courage that steps toward someone's pain rather than stepping around it. Every small act of courage plants a seed in another person's heart. It gives them the strength to face their own fear. It reassures them that they are not alone.

The deepest marks, however, often come from those who have suffered. There is a unique tenderness in a person who has walked through sorrow and allowed God to meet them there. Wounds surrendered to God become wells of compassion that others can drink from. Someone who has lost a child can sit with another parent's grief in a way no one else can. Someone who has buried a spouse understands the ache that lingers in the quiet hours of the night. Someone who has been betrayed can recognize the silent shadows in another person's eyes.

These individuals may not feel strong, but the compassion that has grown in them becomes a gift to the world — a legacy carved from suffering transformed by grace. Their presence comforts others in ways words alone cannot.

Forgiveness leaves a mark, too. When we forgive someone who hurt us deeply, we break the cycle of pain that might otherwise continue for generations. Forgiveness becomes a quiet testimony of God at work in the human heart. And even if the person who hurt us never understands the depth of that forgiveness, others will. People remember when mercy triumphs over bitterness. They remember when grace wins.

But perhaps the most overlooked mark of all is faithfulness. The steady, daily faithfulness that happens away from applause and outside of anyone's recognition.

The prayers whispered on behalf of children or grandchildren. The gentle encouragement offered to a coworker. The compassion extended to a stranger. The consistency of showing up for people who rely on us. These small choices accumulate over a lifetime, creating a legacy far more enduring than dramatic achievements.

A life lived in the pattern Jesus revealed — chosen, blessed, broken, shared — becomes a life that naturally leaves a mark. Not because it seeks attention, but because it quietly reflects the love of Christ in every season. A person who lives this pattern becomes a source of strength for the weary, a safe place for the hurting, a reminder of God's presence for those who feel forgotten.

You may never know how deeply your life has impacted someone. You may never hear the full story. You may never learn how your kindness changed the direction of someone's day or how your compassion gave someone courage. But God knows. He sees every gentle offering. He gathers every act of love. And He multiplies it in ways that reach far beyond your sight.

The mark you leave is not measured by recognition or achievements. It is measured by love. The love you give freely. The love you share quietly. The love that pours out through your life because God first poured it into you.

Every day you live the pattern, you leave a trail of grace behind you — a trail that others can follow when they are searching for hope. A life shared becomes a life that endures, not because of its greatness, but because of its goodness.

Jesus showed us the way.

You are living it every time you give your life away in love.

CHAPTER ELEVEN
When the Road Gets Hard

Every Christian eventually walks through seasons when faith feels heavier than usual. Moments when life is confusing, when prayers seem unanswered, when old wounds resurface, or when the weight of daily struggles presses down with more force than we expected. These seasons can feel disorienting. They can make us question our progress, doubt our calling, or wonder whether God is still guiding us.

Yet the pattern Jesus revealed at the table does not dissolve in difficult seasons. In fact, it is often in those very moments that the pattern becomes clearest. When life grows heavy, the steady truth beneath us does not shift. We remain chosen, blessed, broken in honest ways, and capable of being shared even when our strength feels small.

Difficult seasons sometimes cause us to forget the first movement — that we are chosen. When life feels uncertain or discouraging, we may assume God has stepped back or that His plans for us have changed. But God's choosing is not fragile. It does not weaken when we are overwhelmed.

It does not disappear when our faith feels thin. The same hands that took the bread continue to hold us, even when we tremble.

During hard seasons, we often fail to notice the blessing movement as well. Blessing in easy times feels bright and obvious. Blessing in difficult times can feel hidden — not gone, but quieter. Sometimes the blessing is the strength that carries us through one more day. Sometimes it is a person God places in our path at the right moment. Sometimes it is a comfort we feel in prayer, or a verse that steadies our spirit, or peace that arrives unexpectedly in the middle of chaos. Blessing is not absent in difficulty; it simply takes on a different shape.

These seasons also bring us into deeper contact with our brokenness. Not through shame or failure, but through the simple truth that hardship exposes our needs. During these times, we often realize how limited our own strength is. We notice cracks in our patience, our confidence, or our ability to cope. We become aware of our fears and insecurities. And while this can feel discouraging, it is often where God's grace shines most clearly. God meets us in these cracks, not to condemn us, but to hold what we cannot hold ourselves.

Difficult seasons also have a way of stirring old wounds — losses we've carried for years, disappointments we thought we had moved past, grief that remains tender. When these wounds resurface, we may wonder why they still have such power. But wounds returning are not signs of failure; they are invitations. Invitations to let grace heal new layers of a story we are still living. Healing rarely happens all at once. It comes in gentle waves, often in moments we don't expect.

There is something sacred about the way God moves in us during these times. We may feel fragile, but God is steady. We may feel unsure, but God is faithful. We may feel as though we have nothing to offer, but even the smallest act of love — given from a weary heart — carries more weight than we realize. A comforting word spoken from a place of struggle can hold more authenticity than a polished sermon. A prayer whispered through tears can carry more honesty than a prayer offered with ease. When we share from a place of vulnerability, God uses our lives in quiet but meaningful ways.

One of the surprises of the shared life is how often God works through us while He is also working within us. Many people believe they must be strong before they can be useful. But God often uses people who feel weary, unsure, or inadequate. In fact, the times when we feel weakest are often the very times when our compassion is deepest. We understand others more clearly because we are walking through something similar. Our words become gentler, our presence more sincere, our hearts more open.

There is comfort in remembering that Jesus Himself understood difficult seasons. He knew hunger, fatigue, loneliness, disappointment, and grief. He wept at a friend's tomb. He felt the sting of betrayal. He prayed in anguish. Our Savior was not untouched by hardship — He walked through it with us and before us. And because He did, we can trust His presence in every moment of our own pain.

Difficult seasons also teach us something about dependence. When life feels manageable, it is easy to believe we are carrying ourselves. When the road grows hard, we remember who truly carries us. We lean more deeply into prayer. We reach more willingly for God's peace. We rediscover the comfort of Scripture. And sometimes, without realizing it, we grow in ways that hardship alone can shape. Strength forms. Compassion deepens. Faith expands. Trust becomes more personal.

These seasons also draw us toward others. We learn to reach out when we need support. We learn that there is courage in asking for prayer, honesty in admitting we are struggling, and humility in letting someone walk beside us. Community becomes a shelter instead of a formality. When people step into our lives during these times — not with quick solutions, but with presence — they become living reminders of God's nearness.

And even when life feels heavy, we remain capable of being shared. Not in grand, impressive ways, but in simple, quiet ones. A smile offered to someone else who is hurting. A gentle word spoken from a place of empathy. A moment of patience when frustration would have been easier. These small acts become gifts to others, especially because they come from a heart that understands struggle.

Hardship never removes us from God's story. More

often, it deepens our role in it. Seasons of difficulty refine us. They soften what needs softening and strengthen what needs strengthening. They prepare us to be more compassionate, more understanding, more patient, and more generous with our lives. They shape our hearts into the kind of hearts that reflect Christ — not through perfection, but through presence.

If you are walking through a hard season now, remember this: nothing about your struggle disqualifies you from grace. Nothing about your circumstance alters your identity. You are still chosen. You are still blessed. You are still being held, even in your brokenness. And you still have a life that God can use — right now, exactly as it is.

The pattern holds in every season.

Especially the difficult ones.

And God walks each step with you.

CHAPTER TWELVE
A Rhythm That Shapes the Heart

By now, the pattern of the Lord's Supper has become more than an idea on a page. It has begun to take on a life of its own. It threads itself through our days, rises gently in our thoughts, and becomes a steady reminder of who we are and how God works within us. What Jesus revealed in a single sacred moment becomes a rhythm that can guide an entire lifetime.

Most spiritual growth does not happen in sudden leaps. It happens slowly, quietly, almost invisibly, through rhythms that become part of us over time. The more we return to the pattern — chosen, blessed, broken, shared — the more deeply it roots itself in our hearts. It becomes a lens through which we see ourselves, others, and God. It becomes a pathway we follow even when we are not consciously thinking about it.

We begin noticing the "chosen" movement in moments that once seemed ordinary. A verse that speaks directly to the heart. A sense of peace that arrives unexpectedly. A conversation that gently reminds us of our worth. These small moments become reminders that God is still calling your name, still shaping your story, still writing purpose into the pages of your life.

We begin noticing the "blessed" movement as well, not only in the good times but in the quiet, sustaining grace that carries us through days that feel uncertain. We find ourselves whispering prayers of gratitude in moments we once rushed past. We begin thanking God not only for what is going well, but for the strength that sustains us when things are difficult. Blessing becomes less about what we receive and more about who walks with us.

We begin noticing the "broken and wounded" movement with new humility and compassion. Instead of hiding our flaws, we acknowledge them more honestly. Instead of berating ourselves for our weaknesses, we allow God's mercy to meet us there. We recognize our wounds not as signs of failure but as places where God has been faithful. And as we become more honest with ourselves, we grow more patient with others. We begin to understand that everyone carries something hidden, something heavy, something that needs gentleness.

And then comes the "shared" movement — the place where the pattern takes on its fullest expression. We start to sense God inviting us to share not only our strengths but our struggles. We discover that our best moments of ministry often rise from the places where we once felt the weakest. We find ourselves offering encouragement more freely. We notice the people around us who need kindness.

We become more willing to reach out, to listen, to support, to walk alongside. And slowly, almost without realizing it, our lives begin to pour outward.

When these movements become part of our daily rhythm, the Christian life feels less like a list of expectations and more like a conversation with God. We stop trying to earn His approval and begin responding to His love. We stop trying to perfect ourselves and begin trusting His work within us. We stop seeing our brokenness as disqualifying and begin seeing it as the place where grace becomes real.

This rhythm also changes the way we see others. Instead of seeing people as obstacles, irritations, or strangers, we begin to see them as stories — stories that God is writing, stories filled with both beauty and pain. The driver who cuts us off may be rushing to a doctor's appointment they are afraid to attend. The coworker who snaps at us may be carrying a grief they cannot articulate. The lonely person in the pew may be longing for someone to notice them. When we see others through the lens of compassion, the shared life becomes second nature.

We also become more aware of our dependence on God. The pattern teaches us that we cannot choose ourselves, we cannot bless ourselves, we cannot heal our own brokenness, and we cannot fully share ourselves without God's guidance. Each movement draws us back to Him. Each movement reminds us that He is the One who shapes and sustains our lives.

This rhythm does not eliminate hardship. It does not shield us from pain. But it gives us a way to move through those experiences with purpose and hope. When difficulties arise, we remember we are still chosen. When we feel empty, we remember we are still blessed. When we face our brokenness, we remember grace meets us there. And when we feel unsteady, we remember that even our smallest acts of love can change someone else's day.

There is a deep peace that comes from living in a rhythm rather than striving for a result. A rhythm is not something you accomplish; it is something you return to again and again. It is something that carries you when you feel strong and sustains you when you feel weak. It is something you learn to trust because it does not depend on your performance.

The pattern Jesus gave us is more than symbolic. It is deeply personal. It invites us to embrace our identity, to receive God's blessing, to face our brokenness honestly, and to offer our lives as gifts to others. It invites us into freedom — not the freedom of being flawless, but the freedom of being loved.

In time, you may notice that this rhythm begins to change you in ways you did not expect. You may find more patience rising in your heart. You may feel more tenderness toward people who once frustrated you. You may find the courage to speak honestly or gently in moments that once silenced you. You may feel a growing sense of peace, even in seasons of uncertainty. These changes are not the result of effort alone; they are signs that the pattern has taken root within you.

And as the pattern becomes part of you, something else happens. Others begin to experience it through you. They feel chosen when you speak to them with acceptance. They feel blessed when you offer kindness. They feel safe enough to name their own brokenness. And when your life pours outward in love, they feel the touch of God's presence, sometimes without ever knowing why.

The rhythm shapes you, and through you, it shapes the world.

CHAPTER THIRTEEN
Your Life Has a Calling

As the pattern settles deeper into your heart, something begins to rise within you — an awareness that this is not simply a rhythm you practice. It is a calling. It is the shape of your life's purpose. It is the way God ministers to the world through ordinary people whose stories have been touched by grace.

Many Christians spend years wondering what God wants from them. They search for a grand mission, a clear assignment, or a specific role that will reveal their purpose. Some wait for a moment of clarity that never arrives. Others believe their calling must look dramatic or impressive, something large enough to justify the idea that God has chosen them.

But calling rarely appears with fanfare. It often begins quietly, in the places where God has already been forming your heart. In the places where you have struggled. In the places where you have received mercy. In the places where you have felt broken and discovered healing. God rarely wastes the parts of our story that have shaped us the most.

He often uses them to guide us toward the people who need what our lives have learned.

Your calling is not separate from the pattern — it flows directly out of it.

When you understand that you are chosen, you begin to realize that your life carries intentionality. God saw something in you worth pursuing long before you saw anything in yourself worth offering. He placed your story within His own. He wove your life into the world with purpose. You were chosen not only to be loved but to become an expression of that love.

When you understand that you are blessed, your calling no longer feels like pressure. You do not step into it out of obligation or fear. You step into it out of gratitude. You recognize that everything God has poured into your life — every moment of strength, every whisper of peace, every breath of grace — becomes part of what you now offer to others. You serve not because you must, but because you have been given so much that it naturally spills over.

When you understand your brokenness, your calling becomes more real, not less. You no longer think you need to be perfect to be used. You know that God works in honest hearts, not flawless ones. Brokenness deepens your compassion, sharpens your awareness of others, and keeps you humble in your service. You begin to sense that your struggles have given you insight, empathy, and tenderness that someone else desperately needs.

When you understand that your life is meant to be shared, your calling becomes active. You feel nudges to reach out to someone. You notice opportunities to speak hope. You find yourself being drawn into conversations you once would have avoided. You begin listening in new ways, responding in new ways, and trusting God to guide you in moments that arise unexpectedly. You become more attentive to the quiet invitations God places in your path.

Your calling may not involve a title or a formal ministry. It may not involve a stage or a microphone. In fact, the most meaningful callings often unfold far from public view. A mentor who quietly shapes a young person's life. A friend who walks faithfully beside someone who is grieving. A believer who comforts those who suffer because they have been on that road themselves. A neighbor whose kindness becomes a refuge for lonely hearts. A parent whose steady love becomes the foundation of a child's faith.

These expressions of calling may not seem spectacular, but they hold profound significance in God's kingdom. Calling is not measured by visibility; it is measured by love. It is measured by faithfulness. It is measured by the willingness to allow one's life to be poured out in whatever ways God chooses.

Even when your calling feels small, it is never insignificant. God often works most powerfully through the moments we overlook — the moments that feel ordinary to us but extraordinary to someone else. A phone call placed at the right time. A prayer offered in quiet sincerity. A conversation that gives someone the courage to take the next step. A gentle word spoken on a difficult day.

Sometimes your calling becomes clear through your wounds. If you have endured a loss, you carry a depth of compassion that others need. If you have overcome a recurring sin, you carry insight and grace for those who are still fighting. If you have survived hardship, you carry hope for those who feel helpless. God never wastes pain. He transforms it, and then He places people in your path who need the very comfort you received.

Other times, your calling emerges through your blessings. A gift for listening. A heart for service. A desire to encourage. A natural warmth that draws others in. These blessings are not random; they are intentional parts of how God designed you to reflect His love.

And sometimes your calling simply unfolds through your presence — your willingness to show up, to care, to remain steady, to stay faithful. A person who is present in someone else's life becomes a living expression of God's heart. Presence is often the greatest gift you can offer.

Living your calling does not mean striving to do something great. It means letting God do something meaningful through you. It means paying attention to the nudges of the Spirit. It means trusting that your life — your whole life, with all its beauty and brokenness — has value in God's hands.

When you embrace the pattern, calling becomes less

about finding the "right role" and more about becoming the right heart. A heart that listens. A heart that cares. A heart shaped by mercy. A heart willing to be shared.

You may never know the full impact of your calling this side of heaven. You may never see the seeds that took root, the lives that changed, the hope that blossomed because of a simple act of love you offered. But God sees it all. And in His kingdom, nothing given in love is ever wasted.

Your life has a calling:

Not someday, but now.

Not once you have everything together, but in the midst of your journey.

Not because you are extraordinary, but because God's love is.

The pattern reveals it.

Grace sustains it.

And the world needs it.

CHAPTER FOURTEEN

Being at the Table Is Only the Beginning

When Jesus gathered His disciples on the night of the Last Supper, He was not simply closing a chapter of His ministry. He was beginning one. Being at the table was never meant to be the end of the story. It was only the beginning. It was the doorway into a new way of living, a new way of loving, a new way of being present in the world. What He revealed in those moments was not just a ritual to be remembered, but a pattern to be lived.

Being at the table was only the beginning.

For many believers, the Lord's Supper is something we observe with reverence, gratitude, and devotion. Yet the moment we step outside the walls of our church, life rushes back in — responsibilities, worries, routines. We often separate the sacred from the ordinary, as if the table belongs only to Sunday and the rest of life belongs to Monday through Saturday. But Jesus never separated the two. He gave us the pattern at the table so we would carry it into every part of our lives.

The pattern becomes real not when we understand it, but when we live it.

We live it when we remember, each morning, that we are chosen. Not by accident. Not by default. Chosen with care, purpose, and intention. The God who formed galaxies chose you to bear His love into the world. You carry a divine calling woven into the details of your daily life. Every breath you take, every interaction you have, every person you encounter happens within the story of being chosen.

We live it when we recognize our blessings, even in small and quiet forms. When we see God's goodness in the unexpected — in a friend's kindness, in a peaceful moment, in strength that appears when you feel empty, in a promise from Scripture that settles your spirit. Blessing is not always loud; most often, it arrives in gentle touches. And when you recognize those touches, gratitude softens your heart and opens your hands.

We live it when we face our brokenness honestly. Not with shame, not with self-condemnation, but with the courage that comes from knowing God is merciful. Your brokenness does not define you; it connects you to others. It keeps you humble. It opens the door to compassion. It helps you understand that everyone you meet carries a story that is deeper than what you see.

We live it when we acknowledge our woundedness with tenderness. Some wounds were caused by others, some by life's cruelty, and some by events we never wanted and never deserved. These wounds shape us, but they do not imprison us. When we allow God to meet us there, healing becomes possible. And our wounds — surprisingly and beautifully — become places where others find comfort through us.

We live it when we allow our lives to be shared. When we extend kindness without being asked. When we speak gently to someone who is hurting. When we make room for someone's story. When we reach out to someone who feels alone. When we see the people around us not as strangers but as fellow travelers who need encouragement, hope, and companionship.

This is the rhythm Jesus gave us.

This is the pattern that shapes the Christian life.

This is the way the world is changed.

The pattern is not complicated, though it is profoundly deep. It does not require advanced learning or extraordinary gifting. It requires attentiveness. It requires openness. It requires a willingness to let God work through everyday moments. The pattern turns ordinary days into sacred opportunities.

You may never perform miracles, preach sermons, write books, or lead ministries. But you can sit with someone who is hurting. You can offer encouragement to someone who feels discouraged. You can tell the truth about your own journey. You can be present in someone else's story. And in doing so, you live out the pattern with more authenticity than any public accomplishment ever could.

At the table, Jesus broke bread.

In your life, He breaks open your story.

At the table, Jesus blessed the bread.

In your life, He blesses you in ways you sometimes notice and sometimes miss.

At the table, Jesus shared the bread.

In your life, He invites you to share your heart, your compassion, your time, your presence.

This is not symbolic. This is not abstract. This is love — expressed, embodied, lived.

And as this pattern becomes part of you, something beautiful happens. You begin to recognize it everywhere. You see it in the faces of those who have helped you. You see it in the kindness of strangers. You see it in the resilience of people who have walked through loss. You see it in communities that carry one another through hardship. You see it in the gentle ways God meets you when you feel weak.

The pattern is not only yours to live; it is yours to witness in others as well.

Once you begin to see it, you cannot unsee it.

The world is aching for this kind of life. Not louder faith, but deeper faith. Not more information about God, but more demonstrations of God's love. Not polished perfection, but shared humanity warmed by grace.

The world needs people who are willing to carry the pattern beyond the table and into the places where people feel forgotten or afraid. Into workplaces, neighborhoods, families, friendships, and everyday conversations. Into grief. Into joy. Into ordinary routines. Into messy situations. Into quiet moments no one else sees.

The table is only the beginning.

The real work happens after we rise.

As you finish this book, you are not reaching the end of an idea. You are stepping into a way of living that has power to transform your heart and the hearts of others. Not all at once, and not through dramatic changes, but through steady, daily expressions of the pattern Jesus revealed.

You are chosen.

You are blessed.

You are broken and wounded in ways that do not diminish you.

And you are meant to be shared.

Carry this into your life.

Carry it into your relationships.

Carry it into your places of fear.

Carry it into your moments of joy.

Carry it into the lives of the people who quietly wait for hope.

Let your life speak the pattern with sincerity.

Let your story become a gift.

Let your days — each one — begin to look like the love Jesus offered at that sacred table.

The world needs what God is shaping in you.

And your journey is just beginning.

Epilogue
*The Pattern Continues***

The final words of this book are not meant to close anything. They are simply a pause — a breath — before you continue the journey Jesus began at the table.

The pattern you carry now — chosen, blessed, broken, and shared — will unfold in ways you cannot predict. Some days it will feel natural. Other days it will feel challenging. But every day, it will remain true.

Wherever your story takes you next, God goes with you.

Wherever you feel unsure, His mercy steadies your steps.

Wherever you offer your life in love, His presence becomes visible through you.

Being at the table is only the beginning.

The rest of the story is yours to live.

Walk gently.

Love freely.

Share generously.

And trust that God will use every part of your life — even the parts you once wished to hide — to bring hope into a world longing for grace.

The pattern is already at work in you.

Let it continue.
Amen.

Small-Group Discussion Guide

Every question is designed to open conversation, build trust, and help participants hear one another's stories while reflecting on the book's themes.

1. Chosen

When in your life have you most clearly felt "chosen" by God?

What makes it hard to believe that God chose you personally?

How might seeing yourself as "chosen" change the way you approach daily life?

2. Blessed

What everyday blessings do you overlook most often?

How has God's blessing shown up in quiet or unexpected ways?

How is gratitude shaping — or reshaping — your view of God?

3. Broken

What fears or hesitations do you feel when you think about admitting your brokenness?

Why do you think God uses imperfect people so powerfully?

How has someone else's honesty about their brokenness helped you in your faith?

4. Wounded

What kinds of wounds (loss, grief, betrayal, hardship) have shaped your spiritual journey?

How does God meet us differently in our wounds than in our strengths?

What have your wounds taught you about compassion for others?

5. Shared

Who has "shared their life" with you in meaningful ways?

What keeps you from sharing your story more freely?

What is one small, practical way you can share yourself with someone this week?

6. The Pattern in Everyday Life

Which movement of the pattern is easiest for you to live? Which is hardest?

How might this pattern change your relationships, your home, your friendships, your church community?

Where do you see this pattern at work in the lives of others?

7. Trust, Vulnerability, and Community

What role does vulnerability play in deep Christian friendship?

How can we create safer, more compassionate environments in our churches?

What have you learned from hearing others share honestly?

8. Moving Forward

After reading this book, what is one takeaway that stands out to you?

What is one change — even a small one — you would like God to help you make?

How can your group support one another as each person begins living the pattern more intentionally?

About the Author

J. Brian Pusateri is a Christian author, speaker, and founder of Broken Door Ministries. A lifelong Catholic, Brian's life was profoundly changed during an eight-day silent retreat in 2011, when he experienced a powerful call from God to share a message of mercy, healing, and unconditional love.

Since that time, Brian has been reaching people across the country and around the world through his weekly 4th Day Letters, podcasts, talks, and the Blessed, Broken, and Scared retreat. He is also the author of Blessed, Broken, and Scared: Becoming Eucharist for a Starving World.

In 2014, Brian was temporarily blinded and diagnosed with the rare neurological condition MOG Antibody Disease. This unexpected cross deepened his faith and strengthened his commitment to helping others live with honesty, hope, and trust in God's mercy.

Brian and his wife will celebrate their 50th anniversary this year and enjoy living in the South Carolina mountains, surrounded by God's beauty.

To learn more, go to: brokendoorministries.com